COLOUR AND LEARN ABOUT GOD

GOD IS KIND

God is kind

He gives us food every day. "Give us each day our daily bread." Luke 11:3

God

— — —

kind

— — — —

food

— — — —

Page 2 Key words:

God

kind

food

God is kind

He gives us water to drink. "For I will pour water on the thirsty land, and streams on the dry ground." Isaiah 44:3

water

— — — — —

thirsty

— — — — — — —

dry

— — —

Page 4 Key words:

water

thirsty

dry

Go over the words you have learnt so far:

God
kind
food
water
thirsty
dry

God is kind

He gives us sunny days to enjoy. "He who appoints the sun to shine by day... the Lord Almighty is his name." Jeremiah 31:35

sunny

— — — — —

Lord

— — — —

Almighty

— — — — — — — —

Page 6 Key words:

sunny

Lord

Almighty

Go over the words you have learnt so far:

God   sunny
kind   Lord
food   Almighty
water
thirsty
dry

God is kind

He gives us our family. "God sets the lonely in families." Psalm 68:6

gives

_ _ _ _ _

family

_ _ _ _ _ _

lonely

_ _ _ _ _ _

Page 8 Key words:

gives

family

lonely

Go over the words you have learnt so far:

God	sunny
kind	Lord
food	Almighty
water	gives
thirsty	family
dry	lonely

God is kind

He has given us the Bible to help us. "The Lord announced his word." Psalm 68:11

Bible

_ _ _ _ _

help

_ _ _ _

word

_ _ _ _

Page 10 Key words:
Bible
help
word

Go over the words you have learnt so far:

God	sunny	Bible
kind	Lord	help
food	Almighty	word
water	gives	
thirsty	family	
dry	lonely	

God is kind

He gives a beautiful life in heaven, to those who love him. "For the wages of sin is death but the gift of God is eternal life in Jesus Christ our Lord." Romans 6:23

heaven

_ _ _ _ _ _

gift

_ _ _ _

Jesus

_ _ _ _ _

Page 12 Key words:

heaven

gift

Jesus

Go over the words you have learnt so far:

God	sunny	Bible
kind	Lord	help
food	Almighty	word
water	gives	heaven
thirsty	family	gift
dry	lonely	Jesus

These are all the words that you have learnt in this book. Try and fit them into the gaps in the following story to see how well you have learnt them.

	thirsty	gives	word
God	dry	family	heaven
kind	sunny	lonely	gift
food	Lord	Bible	Jesus
water	Almighty	help	

_ _ _ is very _ _ _ _. He gives us _ _ _ _ to eat and _ _ _ _ _ to drink. When we are _ _ _ _ _ _ _ and it is a _ _ _ and _ _ _ _ _ day we are glad to drink a cool glass of water. It is God the _ _ _ _ who gives us this glass of water. He is called the _ _ _ _ _ _ _ _ because he is so powerful. He is also very kind and _ _ _ _ _ us lots of things. He gives us our _ _ _ _ _ _ .

He helps __ __ __ __ __ __ people by giving them friends and families. God is so kind that he has given us the __ __ __ __ __ to __ __ __ __ us to obey him. This is called the __ __ __ __ of God. God is so kind that if we trust in Jesus Christ he will allow us to come and live in __ __ __ __ __ __ with him when we die. God will give you the __ __ __ __ of eternal life, life that lasts for ever, if you love __ __ __ __ __ Christ.